WEREWOLF ATTACK!

John Townsend

🌱 Crabtree Publishing Company

www.crabtreebooks.com

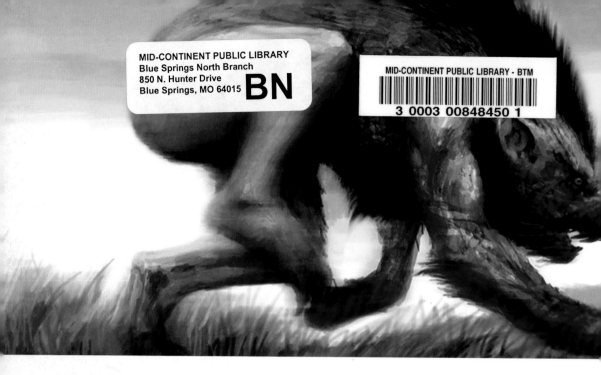

Crabtree Publishing Company

www.crabtreebooks.com   1-800-387-7650

Author: John Townsend
Project editor: Ruth Owen
Project designer: Sara Greasley
Photo research: Lizzie Knowles
Proofreaders: Crystal Sikkens
Production coordinator:
  Katherine Kantor
Prepress technicians:
  Katherine Kantor, Ken Wright

With thanks to series
editors Honor Head
and Jean Coppendale.

Thank you to Lorraine
Petersen and the
members of nasen

**Published
in Canada
Crabtree Publishing**
616 Welland Ave.
St. Catharines, ON
L2M 5V6

**Published in the
United States
Crabtree Publishing**
PMB16A
350 Fifth Ave., Suite 3308
New York, NY 10118

Content development by Shakespeare Squared
www.ShakespeareSquared.com
First published in Great Britain in 2008 by ticktock Media Ltd,
2 Orchard Business Centre, North Farm Road,
Tunbridge Wells, Kent, TN2 3XF
Copyright © ticktock Entertainment Ltd 2008

Picture credits:
Alamy: Mary Evans Picture Library: p. 15 (top); Pictorial Press Ltd.:
  p. 7, 26, 27 (bottom left), 27 (bottom right)
Getty Images: Steve Gorton: p. 22; Christopher Robbins: p. 22;
  Tao-Chuan Yeh/AFP: p. 29
The Bridgeman Art Library: The Beast of Gevaudan, published
  by Basset, 1764 by French School, Musee Nat. des Arts et
  Traditions Populaires, Paris, France/Archives Charmet.
  Illustration by Paul Mudie: cover, p. 9
RGA: American Werewolf Inc: p. 1
Shutterstock: p. 4–5, 12–13, 14, 15 (bottom), 16–17, 19, 20, 21,
  23, 24, 25, 28, 31
SuperStock: Corbis: p. 18
ticktock Media Archive: p. 2–3

Every effort has been made to trace copyright holders, and we apologize in
advance for any omissions. We would be pleased to insert the appropriate
acknowledgments in any subsequent edition of this publication.

Library and Archives Canada Cataloguing in Publication

Townsend, John, 1955-
    Werewolf attack / John Townsend.

(Crabtree contact)
Includes index.
ISBN 978-0-7787-3773-5 (bound).--ISBN 978-0-7787-3795-7 (pbk.)

    1. Werewolves--Juvenile literature. I. Title. II. Series.

GR830.W4T69 2008   j398'.469   C2008-905960-3

Library of Congress Cataloging-in-Publication Data

Townsend, John, 1955-
  Werewolf attack / John Townsend.
    p. cm. -- (Crabtree contact)
  Includes index.
  ISBN-13: 978-0-7787-3795-7 (pbk. : alk. paper)
  ISBN-10: 0-7787-3795-0 (pbk. : alk. paper)
  ISBN-13: 978-0-7787-3773-5 (reinforced library binding : alk. paper)
  ISBN-10: 0-7787-3773-X (reinforced library binding : alk. paper)
  1. Werewolves--Juvenile literature. I. Title. II. Series.

GR830.W4T69 2009
398'.469--dc22

        2008039397

CONTENTS

WEREWOLVES

For thousands of years, people have told stories about scary beasts.

These terrifying stories are about half-human, half-wolf beasts.

These beasts are
called **werewolves**.

WEREWOLF ATTACK

Imagine...
...you are alone in the forest.
The night is very dark.
There are shadows everywhere.

Suddenly, the clouds part.
A full moon shines through
the trees.

A chilling howl fills the night.

You hear a growl behind you.
You feel hot breath on the
back of your neck.

You turn.

You see **fangs** shining
in the moonlight.

The beast attacks you.
There is no escape...

A TERRIFYING CHANGE

You survive the attack. Soon after, you begin to feel strange. Thick hair starts to grow over your body.

Claws grow from your toes and fingers.

You throw back your head and...

...**howl!**

Now you are half-human and half-wolf. You have become a werewolf!

WILD WOLVES

Of course, a human can't really turn into a wolf. So how did these stories start in the first place?

No one knows for sure. But stories about werewolves have been told for thousands of years.

In the past, large numbers of wolves lived wild in many places.

Sometimes food was scarce during bad winters. People had to beware. Hungry wolves might have attacked people.

Maybe people told stories of werewolves because they lived in danger of real wolves.

WOLF BITE

Some werewolf stories may have started because of a disease called **rabies**.

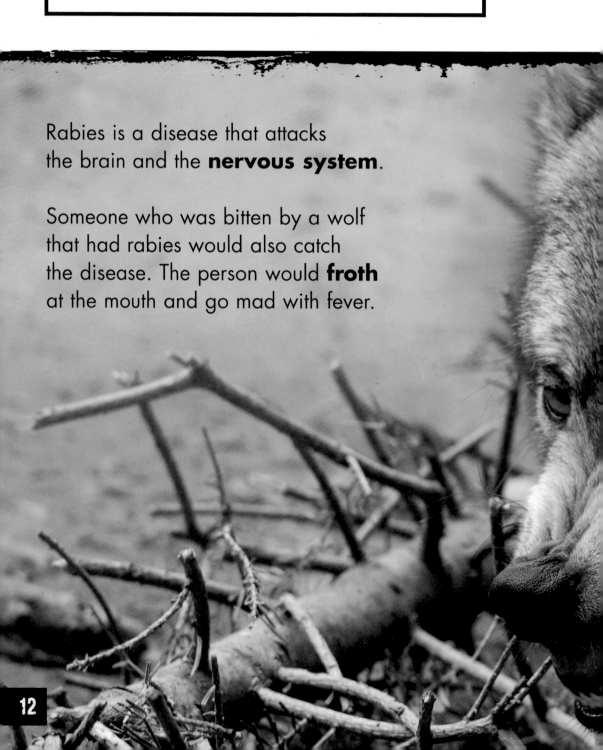

Rabies is a disease that attacks the brain and the **nervous system**.

Someone who was bitten by a wolf that had rabies would also catch the disease. The person would **froth** at the mouth and go mad with fever.

A person with rabies would
act like a wild animal!

In **Viking** times, savage warriors, called Berserkers, wore wolf and bearskin cloaks.

In battle, Berserkers must have looked half human and half animal.

Hundreds of years ago in France, many people believed in werewolves.

Stake

From 1520 to 1630, over 30,000 people were sent to court in werewolf trials. Many people were burnt at the stake for being a werewolf.

Moldy bread

For some people, the problem was their food. They were very poor and only had **moldy** rye bread to eat.

The moldy bread made people ill. It made people grunt and shake and their eyes looked wild.

A FAMOUS LEGEND

The Beast of Gévaudan is a famous French werewolf **legend**.

The Beast of Gévaudan was a huge wolf. It killed around 60 people.

The first attack was in 1765. A woman was chased by a wolf in a forest. Luckily, the beast was driven away by farm workers.

This artwork from the time shows the attack.

Other women and children were not so lucky. The wolf dragged them into the forest and killed them.

People said the beast must have been a werewolf.

THE BEAST OF GÉVAUDAN

Men hunted for the beast. They killed many wolves, but the attacks didn't stop.

After three years of attacks, one hunter finally came face to face with the beast.

The hunter was named Jean Chastel. The legend says that Jean was praying in the forest.

When he looked up...

...he saw the beast!

Jean shot the beast through
the heart with a silver bullet.

The body of the huge wolf
was carried through the town
of Gévaudan to show it was
dead. But legend says it was
not the body of the real beast.

The real body had to be
hidden. It was too frightening
for people to see.

It looked too human!

HOW TO BECOME A WEREWOLF

In the past, people believed there were many ways to become a werewolf.

A bite from a wolf or a werewolf was one way. People also believed you would become a werewolf if you were born on a Friday under a full moon. Or, if you slept with the full moon shining on your face.

Some people believed you would be a werewolf if you had six older brothers and sisters.

The seventh child was **cursed**!

Another belief was that if you drank water from the footprint of a wolf it would turn you into a werewolf.

21

HOW TO SPOT A WEREWOLF

Old stories say there are ways to spot a werewolf.

A person who is a werewolf may have fingers that are all the same length.

They might have hair on the palms of their hands...

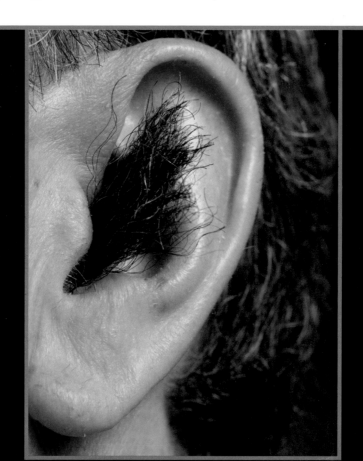

Stories say that a person who is a werewolf
may have eyebrows that join in the middle.

They will also love eating raw meat!

Wolfsbane flowers

Old stories told of ways to destroy werewolves and keep them away.

A poisonous plant called wolfsbane was said to keep werewolves away.

Maybe these stories started because people saw wolves die if they ate wolfsbane.

However, some people believed that eating wolfsbane could actually turn you into a werewolf.

People believed you should try to get three drops of a werewolf's blood. When the blood fell to the ground, the werewolf would turn back into a human.

Most werewolf stories say that the best way to kill a werewolf is with a silver bullet.

MOVIE WEREWOLVES

Werewolf stories are popular. There are many horror movies about werewolves.

In 1981, a movie called *An American Werewolf in London* came out.

In the movie, two young men, Jack and David, are attacked by a savage beast.

David's bones and muscles
bend and change shape.

Jack is killed. David is bitten, but he lives.

However, on the next full moon, David undergoes a terrible change. Movie-goers had not seen such a terrifying change from human to werewolf before.

Special effects make-up artist, Rick Baker, won an award for his work on the movie.

REAL-LIFE WOLFMEN

Some werewolf stories may have started because of rare **medical conditions**.

Some people suffer from a **mental illness** called lycanthropy.

Lycanthropy makes people believe they have turned into a wolf.

Some people are covered in long hair.
They even have hair on their faces and hands.

This extreme hairiness is caused by a condition
called hypertrichosis. The word means "extra ha

This is Jesus Fajardo Aceves from Mexico.
He has hypertrichosis. Other members of
his family also have the condition. But none
of them, of course, is really a werewolf.

NEED-TO-KNOW WORDS

cursed To have harm wished on you, like a bad spell

fangs Long, sharp teeth

froth To produce a lot of foamy, bubbly spit

legend A story from the past. Legends cannot be checked or proved

medical condition An illness or something unusual that affects the body

mental illness A health condition that affects a person's thoughts, emotions, and/or behavior

moldy Covered with a fungus

nervous system Includes the brain, spinal cords, and nerves, and controls the human body

predator An animal that hunts, kills, and eats other animals

rabies A deadly disease that affects the brain. Rabies is spread by the bite of an infected animal

special effects Tricks that movie-makers use to make something seem real in a movie

Viking A warrior from Norway, Denmark, or Sweden. The Vikings invaded parts of Europe 1200 to 900 years ago

werewolf A creature that is half human and half wolf. In Old English the word "were" means "man." Werewolf means "manwolf"

WERE-CREATURES

- Stories of half-animal and half-human creatures are told all around the world.

- In places where there are no wolves, stories of other dangerous, **predator** animals are told.

- In stories from Africa, people turn into hyenas or crocodiles. In old stories from China, people turn into tigers. In Japan, they have stories of werefoxes. In Russia, stories tell of werebears!

WEREWOLVES ONLINE

http://www.everythingwolf.com/wolftalk.aspx
Hear real-life wolf howls and learn about wolf conservation

http://science.howstuffworks.com/werewolf.htm
Information about the history of werewolves